POETS & SAINTS

Participant's Guide

POETS AND SAINTS PARTICIPANT'S GUIDE
Published by David C Cook
4050 Lee Vance View
Colorado Springs, CO 80918 U.S.A.

David C Cook U.K., Kingsway Communications
Eastbourne, East Sussex BN23 6NT, England

The graphic circle C logo is a registered trademark of David C Cook.

The website addresses recommended throughout this book are offered as a
resource to you. These websites are not intended in any way to be or imply an
endorsement on the part of David C Cook, nor do we vouch for their content.

ISBN 978-1-4347-1003-1
eISBN 978-1-4347-1118-2

Published in association with the literary agency of The Fedd Agency, Inc., Austin, TX.

The Team: Alice Crider, Amy Konyndyk, Nick Lee,
Jennifer Lonas, Helen Macdonald, Susan Murdock
Cover Design: Joe Cavazos Design
Cover Photo: Zach Prichard

Printed in the United States of America
First Edition 2016

1 2 3 4 5 6 7 8 9 10

062316

CONTENTS

———————

Poets and saints have inspired us with their books, their poems, their songs, the way they loved, and the way they lived. They must not be forgotten. Their words have stood the test of time and are as important today for us as they were for their contemporaries. Found in their insights are nuggets of truth that through the years have been forged into bonds of iron among the people of God. When we debate with dignity and agree with love, we hold together those sacred convictions that set us apart and cut a path for the return of the King.

—Jamie George, *Poets and Saints*

WELCOME

This *Poets and Saints Participant's Guide* will be your travelogue as you journey through your *Poets and Saints DVD*. Turn to it daily as you meet over the next seven weeks with the fellow travelers in your small group.

Each week will have a different theme as you follow the stories of historical figures, from C. S. Lewis to Saint Francis of Assisi.

Each day of the week will direct you to a different mode of learning meant to move your heart, mind, and spirit to a greater understanding of the way God uses ordinary people to do extraordinary things.

Day 1: *read* the Word of God and focus on what He is saying to you.

Day 2: *pray* the prayer and allow it to inspire your own heartfelt praise and petitions.

Day 3: *reflect* on the lyrics from the corresponding All Sons & Daughters song for the week. To listen to the song, you can access it using the link at the bottom of the page.

Day 4: *look* at the classic work of art and allow it to move you into a space of contemplation with the accompanying commentary and questions.

Day 5: *meditate* on the quotation or ideas and questions provided.

Day 6: *respond* in writing as the text directs you.

Day 7: *learn* as you read the excerpt from Jamie George's book *Poets and Saints* about that week's particular poet or saint to prepare yourself for that day's small-group meeting.

At the end of each week will be a set of discussion points and questions that are to be addressed in your small group following that week's corresponding video.

Enjoy your journey over the next seven weeks. Be open to new ways of thinking and allow God to speak to you as you see Him in the stories of the poets and saints who have come before us.

week one

WILLIAM COWPER AND JOHN NEWTON
EMBRACING LIMITATIONS

————————

John Newton and William Cowper both lived with limitations. Newton lived continually with the regret and shame of being a slave trader. Cowper battled with depression and was at times suicidal throughout his life. Together, however, they faced their fears, pushed through their sadness, and contributed to the love story of God.

Though we might smile and soak up the hope revealed so majestically through the words of the poets and saints who have gone before us, we often forget about the pain and failure in their personal lives. God used Cowper's pain to bring Himself glory. Newton's redemption gave hope to the people he once abused.

Recognize that each limitation in your life can point toward something of value. And remember, a limitation today may not be one tomorrow.

————————

I waited and waited and waited for God.

At last he looked; finally he listened.

He lifted me out of the ditch,

pulled me from deep mud.

He stood me up on a solid rock

to make sure I wouldn't slip.

He taught me how to sing the latest God-song,

a praise-song to our God.

More and more people are seeing this:

they enter the mystery,

abandoning themselves to God.

—Psalm 40:1–3 THE MESSAGE

DEAR FATHER,

WHEN THE DARKNESS OF SHAME COMES OVER ME, PLEASE DRIVE IT AWAY. REMIND ME THAT THE BLOOD OF YOUR SON HAS REDEEMED MY LIFE. GIVE ME EYES TO SEE THE RESTORATION THAT IS TAKING PLACE IN MY LIFE AND GRANT ME THE FAITH TO BELIEVE THAT YOU NEVER CEASE TO MAKE ALL THINGS GOOD. AMEN.

MY ROVING HEART

© 2015 David Leonard, Leslie Jordan

———

Let worldly minds the world pursue

It has no charms for me

Once I admired its trifles, too

But grace has set me free

Its pleasure now no longer please

No more content afford

Far from my heart be the joys like these

Now I have seen the Lord

As by the light of opening day

The stars are all concealed

So earthly pleasures fade away

When Jesus is revealed

Creatures no more divide my choice

I bid them all depart

His name, His love, His gracious voice

Have fixed my roving heart

Now, Lord, I will be Thine alone

And wholly live to Thee

But I may hope that You will own

A worthless soul like me

Yes though of sinners I am the worst

I cannot doubt Thy will

For if Thou had not loved me first

I had refused Thee still

———

🔊 allsonsanddaughters.com/listen

NOTES

Old Man in Sorrow, Vincent van Gogh (1890)

When have you experienced great sorrow? Describe that experience. Were you alone? Were you with a friend or family member? In your time of sorrow, did you feel that God was close or distant?

_____

_____

_____

_____

_____

_____

_____

What do you notice when you see this painting by Van Gogh? What does the man's posture tell you about his story?

_____

_____

_____

_____

_____

_____

_____

As you meditate on this painting, write down your thoughts and feelings.

_____

_____

_____

_____

_____

_____

_____

EXISTENCE IS A STRANGE
BARGAIN. LIFE OWES
US LITTLE; WE OWE IT
EVERYTHING. THE ONLY TRUE
HAPPINESS COMES FROM
SQUANDERING OURSELVES
FOR A PURPOSE.

—William Cowper

RECOGNIZE THAT EACH LIMITATION POINTS TOWARD SOMETHING OF VALUE IN YOUR LIFE. AND REMEMBER, A LIMITATION TODAY MAY NOT BE ONE TOMORROW.

—Jamie George, *Poets and Saints*

EMBRACING LIMITATIONS

Write or draw something creative with your nondominant hand.

William Cowper (pronounced "cooper") was a preacher's kid who became one of England's greatest eighteenth-century writers.

Cowper hailed from a prominent family. His father was the rector of Saint Peter's Church in Berkhampstead, Hertfordshire, England, and his family abounded with lawyers. Cowper was about six years old when his mother died, and he spent his childhood in boarding school, where the older boys abused and molested him. This traumatic childhood experience seemed to lurk in the shadows his entire life.

Having struggled with severe depression for years, probably from his childhood trauma, Cowper had a nervous breakdown in his midtwenties. He was admitted to an insane asylum, where he spent the next two years. Cowper emerged from the mental hospital emotionally frail and continued to battle bouts of depression throughout his lifetime.

After Cowper's stay in the hospital, a local retired clergyman named Morley Unwin and his wife, Mary, took him in. When Morley fell from a horse and died, Cowper moved with Mary to the town of Olney. There he became close friends with the local pastor, John Newton, who had helped Mary and Cowper relocate to a house down the lane from his own.

Cowper developed an unusually close relationship with the older Mrs. Unwin. Living with her in Olney, Cowper dedicated his life to gardening and caring for animals, keeping several rabbits as pets. In light of his emotionally difficult life, it seems that writing was a valuable salve that provided a complementary mélange of self-expression and hope.

Cowper struggled with shame and insecurity for many years. The concept of grace seemed too gratuitous to receive. But one day while sitting in his garden, he sensed the love of God finally breaking through. He wrote, "Immediately I received strength to believe ... and the full beams of the Sun of Righteousness shone upon me. I saw the sufficiency of the atonement [Christ] had made, my pardon sealed in his blood, all the fulness and completeness of his justification. In a moment I believed, and received the gospel."[1]

Newton took great joy in fanning the flame of faith in Cowper's life because he knew what it was like to live apart from the light of Christ.

Newton grew up in a less privileged environment than Cowper. As a rebellious nineteen-year-old, he was press-ganged into the Royal Navy. Eventually Newton found himself in Sierra Leone, where he tried to find employment in the slave trade. Almost penniless, he took a job as a servant to a slave trader but had a miserable experience, suffering abuse and mistreatment along with the slaves. Upon hearing about his son's struggles, Newton's father called on some fellow sailors to retrieve him and return him to England.

On the voyage home, a massive storm erupted, threatening to destroy the ship and everyone on board. There on the Atlantic Ocean, Newton called out to God for deliverance and pledged to dedicate his life to the ways of the Divine. However, like many who choose to follow God, Newton needed time for his understanding of what this meant to materialize.

Newton didn't stay in England long. He found a job as first mate on a slave-trading ship and was eventually promoted to captain. After a number of voyages, he suffered a serious epileptic fit and was advised to quit sailing. Newton did, and after dabbling in a handful of business ventures, he felt drawn to study theology and enter vocational ministry.

As Newton grew closer to God, he began to see clearly the error of his ways, in particular his participation in the dehumanizing practice of human trafficking. Feeling great contrition, he became an important voice in the abolition of slavery in England.

Years later, as a pastor in the small town of Olney, Newton forged a friendship with William Cowper, taking him under his wing. An usual pair, they shared similar backgrounds of redemption and ongoing trust in God that produced great literary insight. Newton and Cowper compiled a collection of songs they had written that were eventually published as the *Olney Hymns*.

Newton and Cowper both lived with limitations. Newton lived continually with the regret and shame of being a slave trader. Cowper battled with depression and was at times suicidal until his death.

Together, however, they faced their fears, pushed through their sadness, and contributed to the love story of God.

WEEK ONE

Discussion Points and Questions

William Cowper and John Newton: Embracing Limitations

William Cowper questioned God and wrestled with internal brokenness throughout his life. In his "sulking house," he found a safe place to speak the truth. Poetry was a way to not only confess struggle but also embrace hope.

1. Do you have a safe place? Where do you go to be alone with your thoughts?

2. John Newton saw in Cowper what Cowper couldn't see in himself. Do you have someone you can confide in? Who has been John Newton in your life? How has that relationship shaped you?

3. Have you had a chance to be John Newton for someone else? What's keeping you from speaking into someone else's life?

4. If John Newton were to stop by your safe place and speak about what he saw in you, what would he say?

5. Read the following: "When you pray, go into your room, close the door and pray to your Father, who is unseen. Then your Father, who sees what is done in secret, will reward you" (Matt. 6:6).

6. Did you know that Jesus is in your safe place and is waiting to whisper what He sees in you? How will understanding this change the way you pray?

NOTES

week two

C. S. LEWIS
VULNERABILITY

———————

C. S. Lewis chronicled the story of Orual, a woman who lives with a veil shrouding her face because she feels great shame from her physical imperfections and shortcomings. A powerful truth is revealed in this great tale: the veil she wears is her fabricated, self-made persona that not only masks her true identity but also acts as a shield that protects her from being truly known by others. Vulnerability doesn't come easy. But when it comes, it brings life.

———————

Whenever someone turns to the Lord, the veil is taken

away. For the Lord is the Spirit, and wherever the

Spirit of the Lord is, there is freedom. So all of us who

have had that veil removed can see and reflect the

glory of the Lord. And the Lord—who is the Spirit—

makes us more and more like him as we are changed

into his glorious image.

—2 Corinthians 3:16–18 NLT

DEAR LORD,

GIVE ME THE COURAGE TO BE HONEST WITH MYSELF, WITH YOU, AND WITH OTHERS. PROMPT ME TO BE VULNERABLE WHEN THE OPPORTUNITY ARISES. SHOW ME WHEN AND WHERE TO RISK WITH LOVE. HERE IN THIS MOMENT, I EXPRESS MY DEEP LOVE FOR YOU AND GRATITUDE FOR INCLUDING ME IN YOUR STORY. AMEN.

HEAVEN MEETS EARTH

© 2015 David Leonard, Leslie Jordan

———————

Oh Light appeared from nothing
Oh Light appeared from nothing
With the Spirit brooding over water
Heaven meets earth

From night then came the morning
From night then came the morning
There was sky in the middle of the water
Heaven meets earth

The sun revealed Your beauty
The sun revealed Your beauty

Every mountain bowing down before You
Heaven meets earth
Creation sings Your glory
Creation sings Your glory
Hallelujahs rising like the daylight
And heaven meets earth

Let all things their Creator bless
And worship Him in humbleness
O praise Him! Alleluia!
Praise, praise the Father, praise the Son
And praise the Spirit, Three in One!

———————

🔊 allsonsanddaughters.com/listen

NOTES

The Creation of Adam, Michelangelo (1512)

Contemplate the moment when God touched Adam—when divinity gave breath to humanity. What do you think that moment was like for Adam? What would it be like to be fully seen and known?

_____

_____

_____

_____

_____

_____

Observe the famous painting from the Sistine Chapel. What do you see? What does God think of His creation? Is He pleased? Does He long for intimacy?

_____

_____

_____

_____

_____

_____

How do you experience God? Has there been a moment in your life where the touch of God felt slightly out of reach because of sin or shame? Did you allow God to see you as you really are in that moment? If no, why not? If yes, what was it like?

_____

_____

_____

_____

———

THERE IS NO SUCH THING AS INSTANT COMMUNITY. A RELATIONSHIP IS AN EXPERIENCE BUILT ON MOMENTS OF RELATING. THE GREATER THE ACCUMULATION AND FLAVOR OF THESE MOMENTS, THE DEEPER THE RELATIONSHIP. THE MORE WE LET GO OF OUR PERFECTIONISM, THE MORE HONEST AND GENUINE THOSE MOMENTS WILL BE.

———

—Jamie George, *Poets and Saints*

When was the last time you caught a glimpse of your true self? How do you think the Creator of the universe sees you, His creation? What might God say to His beloved creation? Today, ask God to help you see yourself the way He sees you.

Born on November 29, 1898, in Belfast, Ireland, Clive Staples Lewis wasn't interested in being a Christ follower and didn't set out to be a Christian apologist or philosopher, as he's known today.

When Lewis was a young man, his mother's death and the alienation of his father diminished any belief he may have had in God. A tutor by the name of W. T. Kirkpatrick introduced Lewis, who was deeply philosophical and an avid reader, to classical literature and taught him to criticize, analyze, and think and write logically. This training reinforced Lewis's decision to be an atheist. With Kirkpatrick's strong tutelage, Lewis was accepted to Oxford University, where he became a student in 1917.

A year later, like most young English men of his time, Lewis served as a soldier in the First World War. After being wounded on Mount Berenchon during the Battle of Arras and becoming disgusted with the boredom and carnage of war, Lewis returned to Oxford to pursue intellectual interests with fervor. He published his first book, *Spirits in Bondage*, in 1919 under the pseudonym Clive Hamilton.

While teaching and writing at Oxford, Lewis conceded that his atheistic worldview was deteriorating. Important questions were met only with inferior answers. He was also beginning to recognize that men of great intellect embraced spirituality. Unable to ignore the Christian wisdom of the ages, he sensed the Spirit of God speaking through poets and saints, including George MacDonald, G. K. Chesterton, John Milton, Julian of Norwich, Saint Augustine, and others. These writers disrupted his pretense and dispelled his disbelief. So Lewis began to look upward and inward.

> *The things I assert most vigorously*
> *are those that I resisted long and accepted late.*
> —C. S. Lewis, *Suprised by Joy*

He resisted God until one night he could resist no longer. He wrote, "You must picture me alone in that room in Magdalen [College], night after night, feeling, whenever my mind lifted even for a second from my work, the steady, unrelenting approach of Him whom I so earnestly desired not to meet. That which I greatly feared had at last come upon me. In the Trinity Term of 1929 I gave in, and admitted that God was God, and knelt and prayed: perhaps, that night, the most dejected and reluctant convert in all England."[2]

As Lewis plunged into a submissive relationship with the Creator, his bright intellect and sociological intuition pushed him to continue to question and interrogate the Christian faith. Believing there was a God was just the first step. He now had to wrestle down the deity of Jesus. At age thirty-three, after a long talk one night with friends, including J. R. R. Tolkien and Hugo Dyson, Lewis accepted that Jesus was indeed the Son of God. For the next sixteen years, along with literature, language, and logic, Lewis discussed faith with his friends and came to understand the impact of the biblical narrative on every facet of life.

In 1956, Lewis married an American writer and former schoolteacher named Joy Davidman. The marriage greatly disrupted the old bachelor's way of life. Joy's two sons provided Lewis with an instant family, just what he needed. In embracing his new life, Lewis shed his self-centered routine. When Joy, whom he was deeply in love with, died of cancer only three years after they married, he was heartbroken.

In his book *A Grief Observed*, Lewis wrote, "God has not been trying an experiment on my faith or love in order to find out their quality. He knew it already. It was I who didn't. In this trial He makes us occupy the dock, the witness box, and the bench all at once. He always knew that my temple was a house of cards. His only way of making me realize the fact was to knock it down."[3]

Throughout Lewis's life, and, in particular, because of Joy's death, he searched for truth. Willing to play his part in the divine production, he also needed to know and be able to trust the character of God.

WEEK TWO

Discussion Points and Questions

C. S. Lewis: Vulnerability

God wants to see us and be seen in us. When we reject our true selves, we cover our faces. We reject the image of God that we uniquely carry and therefore hide that revelation of God from the world, our community, our loved ones, and even ourselves.

1. What veil do you hide behind most frequently?

2. Do you struggle with managing perception? Why?

3. What fears keep you from being yourself in relationships?

4. There is no such thing as instant community. A relationship is an experience built on moments of relating. The greater the accumulation and flavor of these moments, the deeper the connection.

5. What was it like observing Jamie, Leslie, David, and Sarah being vulnerable with one another?

6. Did you get the impression they felt safe with one another? Why?

7. What would we have missed out on as observers if they hadn't trusted one another enough to be vulnerable about their struggles?

8. Does their vulnerability give you permission and courage to be vulnerable? Why, or why not?

9. Read the following: "[The veil] can be removed, as the scripture says about Moses: 'His veil was removed when he turned to the Lord.' Now, 'the Lord' in this passage is the Spirit; and where the Spirit of the Lord is present, there is freedom. All of us, then, reflect the glory of the Lord with uncovered faces; and that same glory, coming from the Lord, who is the Spirit, transforms us into his likeness in an ever greater degree of glory" (2 Cor. 3:16–18 GNT).

10. Vulnerability doesn't come easy. But when it comes, it gives life. And when we're collectively vulnerable, we display a more complete image of God. How could understanding this give you more courage to be vulnerable?

NOTES

GEORGE MACDONALD
SIGNIFICANCE

It seems that some are called to exist as sunlight under the horizon. They have talent. Loads of it. But for whatever reason, their art form inspires other artists rather than the masses.

Some are meant to create art for art's sake. Their artistic renderings carry an elegance—even supremacy. Perhaps this is why the common consumer fails to notice. Without an appreciation for the depth, character, and complexity of the music, the pedestrian will glance, shrug, and disregard the art like a homeowner selling a precious heirloom at a garage sale, unaware of its value.

Though the masses have by no means ignored George MacDonald, the Scottish poet and storyteller from Aberdeenshire, Scotland, a fair share of the uninformed have overlooked him.

Therefore, my beloved brethren, be steadfast [firm],

immovable, always abounding in the work of

the Lord [always being superior, excelling, doing

more than enough in the service of the Lord],

knowing [and being continually aware] that

your toil [labor] is not in vain [it is never futile,

wasted, or without purpose] in the Lord.

—1 Corinthians 15:58 NASB

DEAR JESUS,

YOU SO HUMBLY AND COURAGEOUSLY
LIVED OUT YOUR FATHER'S WILL
AND WERE CONTENT TO FULFILL
HIS PLAN FOR YOU. PLEASE GIVE ME
THE INTEGRITY TO DO THE SAME.
HELP ME NOT TO GET AHEAD OF
YOUR PLAN BUT TO BE PATIENT AND
FIND FULFILLMENT IN YOUR DESIGN
FOR MY LIFE. BECAUSE YOU ALONE
ARE WORTHY OF ALL PRAISE, YOUR
GLORY IS MY AIM AS I CREATE. I WILL
FOLLOW YOU. AMEN.

I WAIT

© 2015 David Leonard, Leslie Jordan, Thomas Jordan

Oh restless heart, do not grow weary
Hold on to faith and wait
The God of love He will not tarry
He is never late

So I wait in the promise
I wait in the hope
I wait in the power
Of God's unending love

Be still and rest secure, my soul
He knows what's best for me
Here in my patience lies the goal
To wait and trust in Thee

Even through my imperfections
His light is shining through
Though dim I am still a reflection
Of mercy and truth

🔊 allsonsanddaughters.com/listen

NOTES

The Mulberry Tree, Vincent van Gogh (1889)

How long does it take a tree to realize its full potential? How long until it reaches the height of its glory and beauty? Does a tree question its purpose, or does it submit to its design, growing in strength and stature?

Does a tree toil for its purpose to be revealed, or does it wait in obedience? What gifts do trees give to creation? Shade? Fruit and sustenance? Flowers and beauty? Shelter and home?

Meditate on these questions as you look at Van Gogh's painting *The Mulberry Tree*: What do you notice about this tree? What gives it meaning? Does creation worship God by simply being?

Write down your thoughts and prayers.

———————

Everyone imagines accomplishing things, and every-one finds him- or herself largely incapable of producing them. Everyone wants to be successful rather than for-gotten, and everyone wants to make a difference in life. But that is beyond the control of any of us. If this life is all there is, then everything will eventually burn up in the death of the sun and no one will even be around to remember anything that has ever happened. Everyone will be forgotten, nothing we do will make any differ-ence, and all good endeavors, even the best, will come to naught. Unless there is God.

———————

—Timothy Keller, *Every Good Endeavor*

Have you ever wondered whether anything you do matters? Have you ever told God that you can't submit to His perfect will for your life?

George MacDonald was born on December 10, 1824, in Aberdeenshire, Scotland. Unlike others in this study, MacDonald had a wonderful relationship with his father and deeply respected him: "From his own father ... he first learned that Fatherhood must be at the core of the universe."[4]

When MacDonald initially attempted to marry his girlfriend, Louisa, he had a very different paternal experience. The young woman's father thwarted their plans because he didn't believe MacDonald was good enough or would be prosperous enough for his daughter. In spite of her father's resistance, Louisa eventually married MacDonald, and they had eleven children together.

MacDonald's first job out of college was pastoring Trinity Congregational Church in Arundel, England. The majority of his congregation loved him. The church leaders, however, being devoted followers of John Calvin's teachings, were endlessly frustrated with him. For one thing, MacDonald didn't agree with Calvin's doctrine of predestination, the belief that only select humans, "the elect" as Calvin called them, could access the grace of God. MacDonald couldn't conceive of a God who didn't offer salvation to all. This theological difference of opinion became a deep source of contention. Only a few years passed when the leadership, in an attempt to manipulate MacDonald into leaving the church, reduced his salary significantly. The underhanded scheme didn't work at first, but eventually, at twenty-nine years of age, MacDonald resigned. Broke and without a job, he was unable to support his growing family. His father-in-law's prophecy seemed to come true.

Division has done more to hide Christ from the view of all men than all the infidelity that has ever been spoken.
—George MacDonald, *Paul Faber, Surgeon*

After leaving the church, MacDonald was unable to land another job immediately, so he pursued writing. His first work, a book-length poem titled *Within and Without*, was published when he was thirty-one. Three years later, in 1858, he published a mythical tale for adults called *Phantastes*. In it the narrator, Anodos, embarks on a journey in fairyland, where he encounters a shadow demon, tree spirits, invisible hands, and a magical castle. The tale's detailed world of enchantment, full of allegory and moral truths, met with great success and catapulted MacDonald's career as a fiction writer.

C. S. Lewis randomly picked up *Phantastes* at a train station one day. After reading it he remarked, "It was as if I were carried sleeping across the frontier, or as if I had died in the old country and could never remember how I came alive in the new ... I did not yet know (and I was long in learning) the name of the new quality, the bright shadow, that rested on the travels of Anodos. I do now. It was Holiness.... It was as though the voice which had called to me from the world's end were now speaking at my side."[5]

MacDonald's influence contributed to Lewis's finding Christ and creating mystical literature of his own. How different the world would have been had Lewis not picked up MacDonald's book that day.

This is a prime example of one man's gift shaping another man's legacy. King Solomon once wrote, "What has been will be again, what has been done will be done again; there is nothing new under the sun."[6] Each person borrows from the inspiration of another, only reframing what others have spoken. And so we must be careful not to take ourselves too seriously.

When you're tempted to think you have little worth or nothing of value to offer, remember this: We're meant to write, sing, sculpt, design, craft, parent, clean, and study in our own way. No one else's. We aren't duplicators; we're interpreters. The goal is never to live someone else's life. We're meant to give back to the world out of our own stories, whatever they may be.

WEEK THREE

Discussion Points and Questions

George MacDonald: Significance

1. What do you find yourself doing that you find impossible not to do? Would you still do it if no one ever noticed?

2. How do you define *significance*?

3. Dallas Willard suggests the following regarding significance: "We were built to count, as water is made to run downhill. We are placed in a specific context to count in ways no one else does. That is our destiny."7

4. Have you ever felt lonely in your pursuit of purpose?

5. Do you share that pursuit, or do you keep it to yourself?

6. As Cara discussed in the video, are you okay being a brick, or do you feel significant only if you're the whole wall?

7. Have you ever experienced successful collaboration? What was it like?

8. Do you wrestle with the question "Does this matter?"

9. Read the following:

You created my inmost being;
    you knit me together in my mother's womb.
I praise you because I am fearfully
    and wonderfully made;
    your works are wonderful,
I know that full well.
My frame was not hidden from you
    when I was made in the secret place,
    when I was woven together in the depths of the earth.

Your eyes saw my unformed body;
    all the days ordained for me were written in your book
    before one of them came to be.
How precious to me are your thoughts, God!
    How vast is the sum of them!
Were I to count them,
    they would outnumber the grains of sand—
    when I awake, I am still with you.
    —Psalm 139:13–18

How does this scripture breathe significance into you?

NOTES

week four

SAINT THÉRÈSE OF LISIEUX
LOVE AND THE LITTLE WAY

———————

Perhaps it was from receiving an abundance of love at home that Thérèse, at such an early age, was able to give her attention to loving God and those in need. Having lost four of their nine children to tragic deaths at young ages, her parents poured their affection into their remaining five daughters. After their mother died, Thérèse's sisters, each in succession, mothered the little girl with utmost devotion. Having such a love modeled for her seemed to form in Thérèse a deep reservoir of love and a great capacity to live a life full of love.

———————

_____

This is how we've come to understand and experience love: Christ sacrificed his life for us. This is why we ought to live sacrificially for our fellow believers, and not just be out for ourselves. If you see some brother or sister in need and have the means to do something about it but turn a cold shoulder and do nothing, what happens to God's love? It disappears. And you made it disappear. My dear children, let's not just talk about love; let's practice real love. This is the only way we'll know we're living truly, living in God's reality. It's also the way to shut down debilitating self-criticism, even when there is something to it. For God is greater than our worried hearts and knows more about us than we do ourselves.

_____

—1 John 3:16–19 THE MESSAGE

O MY GOD! I OFFER THEE ALL MY ACTIONS OF THIS DAY FOR THE INTENTIONS AND FOR THE GLORY OF THE SACRED HEART OF JESUS, I DESIRE TO SANCTIFY EVERY BEAT OF MY HEART, MY EVERY THOUGHT, MY SIMPLEST WORKS, BY UNITING THEM TO ITS INFINITE MERITS; AND I WISH TO MAKE REPARATION FOR MY SINS BY CASTING THEM INTO THE FURNACE OF ITS MERCIFUL LOVE. O MY GOD! I ASK OF THEE FOR MYSELF AND FOR THOSE WHOM I HOLD DEAR, THE GRACE TO FULFIL PERFECTLY THY HOLY WILL, TO ACCEPT FOR LOVE OF THEE THE JOYS AND SORROWS OF THIS PASSING LIFE, SO THAT WE MAY ONE DAY BE UNITED TOGETHER IN HEAVEN FOR ALL ETERNITY. AMEN.

—Saint Thérèse of Lisieux, *The Story of the Soul*

YOU ARE LOVE & LOVE ALONE

© 2015 David Leonard, Leslie Jordan
(Words adapted from Frederic William Farrar, PWP 167)

God and Father, great and holy
Fearing not, we come to Thee and lowly
Fearing not, though weak, lowly
For Your love has set us free

By the blue sky bending over
By the green earth's flowery home
Teach us, Lord, the angel chorus
You are love and love alone!

You are love and love alone
You are love and love alone
You are love and love alone
You are, Lord

Though the worlds in flame should perish
Sun and stars in ruin fall
Trust in Thee our hearts should cherish
Oh, Lord, be our all in all

With Your name the heavens praising
Angels' hymn no sweeter tone
Than the songs our hearts are raising
You are love and love alone

How perfectly
Our hearts are made for love

🔊 allsonsanddaughters.com/listen

NOTES

Field with Poppies, Vincent van Gogh (1890)

Has the thought of living a life devoted to God ever overwhelmed you? Have the big things overshadowed the little things?

_____

_____

_____

_____

_____

_____

_____

_____

_____

_____

_____

Reflect on the prayer from Saint Thérèse on page 53. As you meditate on those words, come back to this painting. Where do you see most of the color? Is it in one small flower or in the many? Write down what you see and how it makes you feel.

_____

_____

_____

_____

_____

_____

_____

_____

_____

_____

_____

_____

———————

I will seek out a means of getting to Heaven by a little

way—very short and very straight, a little way that is

wholly new. We live in an age of inventions; nowadays

the rich need not trouble to climb the stairs, they have

lifts instead. Well, I mean to try and find a lift by which

I may be raised unto God, for I am too tiny to climb the

steep stairway of perfection.... Thine Arms, then, O Jesus,

are the lift which must raise me up even unto Heaven. To

get there I need not grow; on the contrary, I must remain

little, I must become still less.

———————

—Saint Thérèse of Lisieux, *The Story of the Soul*

What are the little things you can do to display love?

_____
_____
_____
_____
_____
_____
_____
_____
_____
_____
_____
_____
_____
_____
_____
_____
_____
_____
_____
_____
_____
_____
_____
_____
_____

Think of a family member or friend whom you haven't seen or spoken to recently. Take some time this week to write that person a letter, send an email or text, or perhaps make a phone call. Examine your heart when you engage in the little things that show love.

Born on January 2, 1873, near Normandy, France, Thérèse Martin was a precocious and energetic child, whose family enthusiastically cherished her.

Having suffered a deep and painful blow at the age of four when her mother died of breast cancer, Thérèse later wrote that the first part of her life stopped that day. She had been very close to her mother and longed for a matronly figure to fill those shoes. As a result, she clung to her older sister, Pauline, who would remain a mentoring presence throughout Thérèse's life.

Following the tragic death of his wife, Thérèse's father, Louis, moved the family about sixty miles north to the little town of Lisieux so that the children could be close to their mother's relatives.

Though an earnest zeal for God and a knowledge of the catechism of the Catholic Church filled Thérèse's youth, a great deal of pain also characterized those years of her life. She suffered severely from headaches and bouts of insomnia.

At one point Thérèse was diagnosed with scruples, a psychological illness likened to obsessive-compulsive disorder and marked by pathological guilt about moral and religious issues. She also had a profound sense of empathy and a deep longing for approval. Her hypersensitivity to what others thought about her, combined with her fear of disappointing God, led her to feel despondent and, at times, inconsolable.

With no success treating her condition medically, in great desperation Thérèse and her family continued praying fervently for healing. One day while lying in bed and praying for a cure, Thérèse looked over at a statue of the Virgin Mary. The figure appeared to come alive and smile at her. At that moment the illness vanished.

Three years later, on Christmas Eve in 1886, Thérèse experienced what she called her complete conversion. That day in a final surrender to God, she found a new confidence in her identity in Him. Her questions, doubts, and fears faded away.

Compelled by these profound religious experiences, Thérèse hoped to follow in the footsteps of her beloved sister Pauline, who became a Carmelite nun. At fifteen Thérèse, accompanied by her father, presented herself to the local bishop to request acceptance to the convent. He told her she would be considered, but because she was so young, she would probably have to wait a few years. In the absence of a sincere commitment from the bishop, Thérèse made her mind up to ask the pope himself.

Happy to oblige his daughter, Louis made arrangements for a trip to Rome that included both Thérèse and her sister Celine. When the day arrived for the family's audience before Pope Leo XIII, Thérèse, Louis, Celine, and others standing in line were given specific instructions: they were to listen to the Holy Father but refrain from speaking to him.

In spite of the warning, Thérèse ignored any sense of decorum and, seizing the moment, left her place in line and threw herself at the pope's feet, begging for entrance into the cloistered life of the convent. When she refused to leave, the guards had to physically pick her up and carry her to the door, but not before she heard Leo's hopeful response: "Go—go—you will enter if God wills it."[8]

God willed it. On April 9, 1888, Thérèse was admitted into the Carmelite convent in Lisieux. What she had longed for "since the dawn of reason,"[9] as she put it, had finally become a reality.

Like George MacDonald, Thérèse had an unshakable confidence in God's love. She never seemed to falter in her recognition of God as a loving father of His children.

Thérèse viewed the pathway to God's kingdom not as a long list of heroic or grandiose achievements but rather as a simple expression of kindness. She wrote, "Love proves itself by deeds, so how am I to show my love? Great deeds are forbidden me. The only way I can prove my love is by scattering flowers and these flowers are every little sacrifice, every glance and word, and the doing of the least actions for love."[10]

Living with great restrictions as a nun and dying from tuberculosis at the age of twenty-four, Thérèse never had a chance to accomplish the deeds of greatness most historians herald. Yet her small acts of love have influenced generations of people around the world.

WEEK FOUR

Discussion Points and Questions

Saint Thérèse of Lisieux: Love and the Little Way

1. Describe the moments when you have been loved.

2. What are the little things you can do to display love?

3. Read this quote from Saint Thérèse:

> Love proves itself by deeds, so how am I to show love? Great deeds are forbidden me. The only way I can prove my love is by scattering flowers and these flowers are every little sacrifice, every glance and word, and the doing of the least actions for love.[11]

Who in your life needs to receive a little flower?

4. Read the following: "If we love one another, God lives in us and his love is made complete in us" (1 John 4:12). How would your life and attitude change if you started seeing moments of loving others as a completion of God's love?

5. This week take time to acknowledge and make note of the little acts of love you receive and give away.

NOTES

PARIS, FRANCE
ART AND ARCHITECTURE

————————

The stained glass kaleidoscope on the west portal of Notre-Dame is mesmerizing. The detail, the symmetry, the craftsmanship, and the vision of the cathedral are inspiring with or without the hunchback. Notre-Dame's art and architecture can make any human feel both small and sublime. Imagine what it must have been like eight hundred years ago when this beacon of hope dominated the landscape for miles in every direction.

————————

[Solomon] decorated the house [of the Lord] with

precious stones for beauty.

—2 Chronicles 3:6 NKJV

O GOD, WHOM SAINTS AND ANGELS
DELIGHT TO WORSHIP IN HEAVEN: BE
EVER PRESENT WITH YOUR SERVANTS
WHO SEEK THROUGH ART AND MUSIC
TO PERFECT THE PRAISES OFFERED
BY YOUR PEOPLE ON EARTH; AND
GRANT TO THEM EVEN NOW GLIMPSES
OF YOUR BEAUTY, AND MAKE THEM
WORTHY AT LENGTH TO BEHOLD IT
UNVEILED FOR EVERMORE; THROUGH
JESUS CHRIST OUR LORD. AMEN.

—Prayer for Church Musicians and Artists,
Book of Common Prayer

REFUGE

© 2015 David Leonard, Leslie Jordan, Paul Mabury

———

You are my refuge
You are my hope
Constant and safe
My home

You are my shelter
I will not fear
Even in darkness
You're here

———

🔊 allsonsanddaughters.com/listen

NOTES

Gothic Cathedral, Pieter Neefs

For centuries, churches have been designed and built to evoke a sense of grandeur similar to that of a heavenly Kingdom beyond our comprehension. High ceilings, colorful windows, light beams flooding in from the sun—these mathematical features were designed to elicit a response. How do you see the Kingdom of God reflected in the architecture?

What is the cathedral in Neefs's painting providing for the people?

As you observe this painting, imagine yourself inside the cathedral. How do you feel? Where in this painting would you be? Would you be standing? Would you be kneeling? Write down your thoughts.

The word of GOD came to Solomon saying, "About this Temple you are building—what's important is that you live the way I've set out for you and do what I tell you, following my instructions carefully and obediently. Then I'll complete in you the promise I made to David your father. I'll personally take up my residence among the Israelites—I won't desert my people Israel."

Solomon built and completed The Temple. He paneled the interior walls from floor to ceiling with cedar planks; for flooring he used cypress. The thirty feet at the rear of The Temple he made into an Inner Sanctuary, cedar planks from floor to ceiling—the Holy of Holies. The Main Sanctuary area in front was sixty feet long. The entire interior of The Temple was cedar, with carvings of fruits and flowers. All cedar—none of the stone was exposed.

—1 Kings 6:11–18 THE MESSAGE

Does God need our words in order to be revealed?
Or does He also whisper through a brushstroke?
In a melody?
In carefully arranged and colored glass?
In something we can't explain, something that takes our breath away?
Does He speak through what is simply beautiful?
—Sarah MacIntosh

Color in the image of the stained glass below.

French philosopher Alain de Botton wrote, "In the eyes of medieval man, a cathedral was God's house on earth."[12]

Why are we drawn to these grand accomplishments called cathedrals? Gazing at a cathedral like Notre-Dame inspires us to consider what thing of beauty we might create if we drew in our focus, worked diligently, took the long view, and collaborated charitably with others.

That kind of dreaming is scary. That kind of risk is unnerving. And there, along the underbelly of our visions, lies an unspoken reality.

Sometimes we believe we're better off without beauty. Are there times you don't want to recall sweet memories?

Ever had a moment when you pulled your gaze from a sunset or mountain vista because deep inside you knew the view would come to an end anyway, and in the agony of it all, you decided there would be less pain if you determined the ending rather than letting the ending sneak up on you?

I wonder how many relationships have ended for this very reason.

Beauty is wild. Intimidating. Glorious. It reminds us of the great beyond. That makes us feel sad. And sometimes, that sadness is too much to bear.

According to Botton, "A perplexing consequence of fixing our eyes on an ideal is that it may make us sad. The more beautiful something is, the sadder we risk feeling.... Our sadness won't be of the searing kind but more like a blend of joy and melancholy: joy at the perfection we see before us, melancholy at an awareness of how seldom we are sufficiently blessed to encounter anything of its kind. The flawless object throws into perspective the mediocrity that surrounds it. We are reminded of the way we would wish things always to be and of how incomplete our lives remain."[13]

Sometimes in religious subculture, there's a tendency to use hype as a mechanism for minimization and denial. If we can get pumped up enough, we can forget at least temporarily that life is hard, that we have doubts, that we struggle with sin, and that we're a far cry from Eden. In some circles there's no room for lament. No space for sorrow. If we purpose in our hearts to never experience melancholy, we'll miss out on a great deal of beauty.

Blessed are those who mourn,
for they will be comforted.
—Jesus, Matthew 5:4

We cannot deny the incompleteness we feel in this life. God knows this and, in His creative pursuit, beckons us to stop, look, and listen. He uses more than just words to move our hearts and draw us to Himself. He speaks to us through images, icons, curves, and colors. Of course, like anything else, this can be twisted and misaligned. The medium of art can become an end in itself, and wood and stone can take on the forms of gods. Our fallen nature is unflinching in its determination to find shortcuts to worship.

How do we admire a creation without making it a god? How is faith connected to creating? How do we lean into the tension between what is and what could be?

75

WEEK FIVE

Discussion Points and Questions

Paris, France: Art and Architecture

1. Visually, what caught your attention most in the video?

2. Was it awkward or uncomfortable watching the section of video without words? Why or why not?

3. What feelings did you have while watching the images?

4. Does God need our words to reveal Himself?

5. Describe a moment when you walked into a building and its beauty took your breath away.

6. Describe a time when you looked out over God's creation, and its beauty prompted wonder.

7. What themes are common in art, architecture, and creation?

8. For thousands of years, humans have expressed or experienced emotions through art and architecture. In what art form is it easiest for you to express or experience emotion?

NOTES

SAINT AUGUSTINE OF HIPPO
LONGING AND JOY

Augustine spent three decades seeking love, pleasure, and the meaning of life. He sought to satiate his longings with unbridled sexual
indulgence. He pursued philosophy and logic in an attempt to quell
the haunting whispers of his soul. He adopted different belief systems
in an effort to quench his irrepressible thirst for something more. At
most these pursuits offered only temporary relief. Why?

Why do we have unmet longings woven into our existence? Why do
we ache when true desires, expectations, and needs go unfulfilled?
Perhaps it's because we're designed to be fulfilled.

———————

He has made everything beautiful in its time. He has

also [planted] eternity in the human heart [a divinely

implanted sense of a purpose working through the ages,

which nothing under the sun but God alone can satisfy];

yet no one can fathom [find out] what God has done

from beginning to end.

———————

—Ecclesiastes 3:11

DEAR GOD AND KING,

MY HEART IS RESTLESS. I LONG FOR
THE WORLD TO BE MADE WHOLE AND
FOR ME TO BE SET FREE. I AM TIRED OF
MY STRUGGLE WITH SIN, YET I PRESS
ON. I KNOW THAT IN THE TENSION OF
WHAT IS AND THE PROMISE OF WHAT
WILL BE, I AM BEING MOLDED INTO
THE PERSON YOU WANT ME TO BE.
PLEASE GIVE ME PATIENCE, O LORD,
AS YOU ORDER MY STEPS AND DIRECT
MY PATHS. I TRUST YOU. AMEN.

REST IN YOU

© 2015 David Leonard, Leslie Jordan, Cara Fox

(Words adapted and paraphrased from Saint Augustines Confessions)

Who is Lord, but our Lord
Who is God, only God
You are the highest
You are most good

Matchless is Your love
Our praise will rise above
Your peace like a river
Floods over us

Our hearts are restless
Until they find rest in You
Our hearts are restless
Until they find rest in You

This is where my hope lies
This is where my souls sighs
I will always find my rest in You

So full of mercy
Beauty and mystery
You are most hidden
But always with us

You're always moving
Always pursuing
Ever creating
Yet, You hold it all

You cannot change,
Yet You change everything

🔊 allsonsanddaughters.com/listen

NOTES

The Bench at Saint-Rémy, Vincent van Gogh (1889)

Where do you go to meet with God? A special table at a coffee shop? A small bench in a garden? Or for a walk in the woods? Where do you go when you're longing to hear the gentle whispers of God?

_____

_____

_____

_____

_____

As you recall that sacred place, observe this painting by Van Gogh. Imagine yourself sitting in between the tall trees. Listen to the water splashing in the fountain behind you. Feel the wind rustling through your hair. What makes this bench safe? Is there an ache in your heart to hear from God?

_____

_____

_____

_____

_____

Is it quiet? Write down what you are longing to hear. Is God speaking to you now? Write down what you hear Him saying.

_____

_____

_____

_____

_____

―――――――

Longing is real. Undeniable. I want something. I
yearn for something. Most of the time I'm not even sure
what that something is. Although the older I get, the
more I'm convinced it's connection with the Creator
and His creation.

―――――――

―Jamie George, *Poets and Saints*

Why do we have unmet longings woven into our existence? Why do we ache when true desires, expectations, and needs go unfulfilled?

Augustine was born in AD 354 in North Africa to a pagan Roman official and a devout Christian woman named Monica. Augustine's mother prayed faithfully for her husband and son. During Augustine's adolescence, she admonished him to avoid sex outside of marriage and other forms of sexual immorality. The young man interpreted this as "womanish"[14] advice and set about ignoring it.

At seventeen years of age, Augustine moved to Carthage, Italy, where "outrageous loves," as he described them, wooed his adolescent desires. In this deep emotional and spiritual hunger, he tenaciously sought to satisfy his cravings through a "cauldron of illicit loves."[15] His drunken indulgence of the sensual lifestyle left him with broken relationships and created within him jealousies, anger, and eventually regret and a deep emptiness.

In the midst of his carnal quests, he set about studying the dicipline of rhetoric, the art of elegant and convincing communication. While studying in Carthage, Augustine encountered a book by Cicero titled *Hortensius*. This evoked in Augustine a new passion for the study of philosophy, which, according to Cicero, could be defined as the "love of wisdom."

To clarify, this wasn't a conversion to a new faith but rather a shifting of priorities. Augustine was famous for praying during this time, "God, give me chastity ... but not yet."[16]

At twenty years of age, having completed his studies, Augustine returned home and became a teacher. However, after the death of a friend, he found it unbearable to remain, so he moved back to Carthage, where he opened a school of rhetoric. This venture didn't last long, however. Frustrated with his unruly students, he moved again, this time to Rome, where he plied his trade and sought to dispense his knowledge in this center of world influence. Unfortunately, the Italian students failed to remunerate their teacher. Frustrated again at age thirty, Augustine accepted an invitation to become a professor of rhetoric in Milan. His mother went with him, still praying and hoping that her son would convert to Christianity. Her prayers were answered.

In Milan, Augustine was engrossed in the insight and skill of the city's most famous orator, Ambrose. In him Augustine saw what it looked like to be a Christian as well as an intellectual. Through Ambrose's teachings and his mother's prayers, the truths of Jesus Christ finally met the longing in his soul.

On an autumn day in AD 386, thirty-two-year-old Augustine, agitated in soul and feeling the violence of shame, ran outside his rented home and collapsed in tears under a fig tree. The stories of others finding faith and freedom in God were creating in him a realization of his own self-hatred.

For the first time in his life, Augustine addressed God. "How long, Lord? Will You be angry with me forever?" His despondency was interrupted when he heard a child's voice say, "Take it and read, take it and read."[17] Augustine got up and walked back inside to his gaming table, where he had left a book that contained a collection of the apostle Paul's letters. He found Paul's message to the Romans, and the result has been called "one of the most dramatic conversions to Christ ever recorded."[18]

Contemplating a monastic life, Augustine made arrangements to travel back to North Africa. On the journey, he visited a friend in the port town of Hippo, where local church leaders pressed him into becoming a priest and taking on a congregation. Augustine was reluctant at first but eventually relented. He never moved again. After the local bishop's death, Augustine took his place and served the church faithfully until his death at age seventy-six.

It was in relationship with others, in the dirt of people's lives, that he wrote most of his works, including *Confessions* and *The City of God*, which would make him "the most influential theologian in the entire Latin-speaking church since New Testament times."[19]

WEEK SIX

Discussion Points and Questions

Saint Augustine of Hippo: Longing and Joy

1. How would you define *joy*? Describe what it is like when you are joy-full.

2. Do you believe joy is something you choose? If yes, why do so many of us fail to choose it?

3. Augustine said, "You have made us for Yourself, and our hearts are restless until they find their rest in You."[20] Describe what it is like to have a restless heart.

4. We have a propensity to allow our restlessness to drive us toward addictions and distractions. What are your addictions or distractions of choice?

5. After wrestling with addiction or a season of distraction, what typically draws your focus back to God?

6. Why would God weave unmet longings and restlessness into our existence?

7. In the book of Ecclesiastes, the author wrote, "He has made everything beautiful in its time. He has also set eternity in the human heart; yet no one can fathom what God has done from beginning to end" (3:11). Does this verse give you hope for your eternal longings? Why, or why not?

NOTES

week seven

SAINT FRANCIS OF ASSISI
SURRENDER

———

Saint Francis had an unbending commitment to what he referred to as "Lady Poverty"—not as the end goal but rather a pathway toward maintaining an intimate relationship with Jesus Christ. In his story the combination of excess wealth and pressure from his father provoked his deepest pain and formed his greatest obstacles to peace and fulfillment. In his desire to be deeply known by God and in his determination to avoid the manipulative power of money, Saint Francis sought a life of deprivation.

———

————————

The kingdom of heaven is like treasure hidden in

a field. When a man found it, he hid it again,

and then in his joy went and sold all he had and

bought that field.

————————

—Matthew 13:44

LORD, MAKE ME AN INSTRUMENT OF THY PEACE. WHERE THERE IS HATRED, LET ME SOW LOVE; WHERE THERE IS INJURY, PARDON; WHERE THERE IS DOUBT, FAITH; WHERE THERE IS DESPAIR, HOPE; WHERE THERE IS DARKNESS, LIGHT; WHERE THERE IS SADNESS, JOY. O DIVINE MASTER, GRANT THAT I MAY NOT SO MUCH SEEK TO BE CONSOLED AS TO CONSOLE, TO BE UNDERSTOOD AS TO UNDERSTAND, TO BE LOVED AS TO LOVE; FOR IT IS IN GIVING THAT WE RECEIVE; IT IS IN PARDONING THAT WE ARE PARDONED; IT IS IN DYING THAT WE ARE BORN TO ETERNAL LIFE.

—Saint Francis, "**Peace Prayer**"

I SURRENDER

© 2015 David Leonard, Leslie Jordan, Jason Ingram

———

The riches of this world will fade
The treasures of our God remain
Here I empty myself to owe this world nothing
And find everything in You

I surrender, I surrender
I surrender all to You

Take my life, a sacrifice
In You alone I'm satisfied
Here I empty myself to owe this world nothing
And find everything in You

Not my will, but Yours be done
Not my strength, but Yours alone
Nothing else but You, oh Lord
I find everything in You

———

🔊 allsonsanddaughters.com/listen

NOTES

Sunflowers, Vincent van Gogh (1887)

A sunflower turns its face toward the sun for warmth and nourishment. Not only does it absorb the sun's rays; it also oddly resembles the greatest energy source in the universe, the sun. There are striking similarities. Give attention to the detail in Van Gogh's painting. How do the intricacies in the design of the sunflower imitate the meticulous design of your life?

As you observe this painting, reflect on the character of God. How often do you turn toward the Source? Do you see obedience in the sunflower?

What do you look like when you surrender to God?

———

The true story of every person in this world is not the story you see, the external story. The true story of each person is the journey of his or her heart.

———

—John Eldredge, *The Sacred Romance*

What keeps you distracted? What gets the majority of your attention? Spend time today in silence, turning off your phone, your computer, or whatever else may distract you. Find yourself resting in the presence of God. Listen for His voice. What do you hear?

Named Giovanni di Pietro di Bernardone at birth and later nicknamed Francesco, Francis was born in the late twelfth century in the small Italian town of Assisi. His father, Pietro, a seller of cloths and dyes, was a very successful merchant.

Francis's mother, according to tradition, was a beautiful woman who loved history and literature. She seems to be the one who opened a portal for her son into a world of imagination. From the time he was a child, it is said that she would spin tales of the magnificent conquests of great knights. Like most boys of that era, Francis probably loved the story of Charlemagne. As a young man, Francis dreamed about becoming someone of great significance, someone famous, perhaps even a knight who would inspire children's stories.

To Pietro's great disappointment, Francis made it pretty clear as a teenager that he had no interest in following in his father's footsteps. Rebellious and impertinent, Francis continually tried to pull away from his father and his demanding expectations. However, Francis had great charisma and prolific leadership qualities. Before long he gathered a posse of his friends, who polluted the town with their raucous behavior and drunkenness, wreaking havoc and disturbing the peace.

Pietro was not pleased. He expected his son to be industrious and not waste his time on frivolous pursuits. He didn't refrain from giving Francis money, however, and Francis didn't refrain from spending it.

Still nursing his childhood dream of becoming a knight, the young man hired an instructor who trained him in the art of warfare. Francis's dreams of going to battle came true in his twenties: the fourth crusade called for soldiers, and with about eight other men from Assisi, Francis galloped off to pursue the romance of battle. He had ridden no farther than a day's ride from town when he became ill and fell behind. Alone on his trotting horse, he was surprised to hear a voice.

"Who can do more good for you, the lord or the servant?"

A bit delirious and unsure where the voice was coming from, Francis answered, "The lord, of course!" He didn't have God in mind, however, but a powerful man, such as a landowner or noble.

A follow-up question resonated in the quiet countryside: "Then why are you abandoning the lord for the servant?"[21]

As Francis rode along contemplating these words, his thinking shifted. He finally realized that this was the voice of God and that "the lord" this voice spoke of was the Son of God. Francis immediately turned his horse around and headed back to Assisi. In the face of potential embarrassment, he rode through the familiar streets and retired to his home. Removing his beloved suit of armor, Francis began wrestling with his experience on the road and its deeper meaning.

Six months later, news arrived in town. The region's entire army had been ambushed and massacred. Had Francis remained with his comrades, he would have been killed.

Lost in a quandary over life's purpose and preoccupied with the needs of the poor, Francis no longer found pleasure in his exploits with friends. He determined that unlike his tendencies in the past, he would never again refuse a man who asked something of him, whether time or possessions.

Francis became progressively attuned to the needs of those around him. Through this growing empathy and compassion, he was getting to know the heart of God.

He was also accepting his inadequacy to perform perfectly, recognizing that salvation was found in Christ alone.

Francis was experiencing conversion, a process peppered with experiences that would bring him closer and closer to God. His encounter with a leper solidified his yearning to know the Creator. As Francis tended to the needs of the diseased, the Spirit of God poured through him with a renewed profound love, and Francis was forever transformed.

After seeing a vision from God, Francis felt it was his mission to obey God's voice, so he gave all the money he had to help rebuild a dilapidated local church. The priest was unwilling to take the money, so Francis simply left it on a windowsill and went about his work.

Agitated that Francis had abandoned the family business and angered that his son had given his money to a church, Pietro took Francis to court. When the powers that be dismissed the matter, Pietro approached the town's church leaders and told the bishop that he wanted to formally renounce his son and be repaid every dime that Francis had given away. The bishop agreed to hold a trial and summoned Francis to appear.

Sometime before the trial, the bishop, knowing that Francis had given his money for good works and, in particular, for rebuilding a church, pulled the young man aside and encouraged him to return his father's money. Consequently, just before the official event began, Francis walked up to his father and with hands outstretched gave him back every dime.

But he didn't stop there. On that freezing winter day, Francis also removed all his clothes and, completely naked, handed the rumpled and worn garments to his father, saying, "From now on I can freely say, 'Our Father who art in heaven,' not father Pietro di Bernadone, to whom, behold, I give up, not only the money, but all my clothes too."[22]

Observing the scene from a few feet away, the bishop was touched by this display of strength and nonviolent, direct action. Francis had turned the tables. Rather than let his father shame him, Francis had spoken directly to the deeper issue at hand, giving up literally everything and stripping his dad of authority and control.

There was no triumph for the abusive father. As a matter of fact, if anything, the people took pity on Francis and looked at Pietro as a man without compassion.

As Francis stood exposed in body and soul, the bishop took his mantle off and put it around the young man—not only physically covering Francis's nakedness, but also symbolically transferring dignity and authority. That bishop and other men eventually became mentoring father figures in Francis's life.

The kingdom of heaven is like a merchant looking for fine pearls. When he found one of great value, he went away and sold everything he had and bought it.
— Jesus, Matthew 13:45—46

WEEK SEVEN

Discussion Points and Questions

Saint Francis of Assisi: Surrender

1. Describe a time when you abandoned living a certain way and were rejected for it.

2. Just as the priest covered Francis with his mantle, God covers us. He protects us, removes our shame, and adopts us as sons or daughters. Describe a time when you experienced God nurturing you in this way.

3. Francis's primary goal in life wasn't poverty; his greatest quest was to remain connected to God. He removed material possessions so they wouldn't be a hindrance in that quest. What obstacles get in the way most often between you and God?

4. In what area of your life is it most difficult to surrender control?

5. Larry Crabb writes, "Most people tuck their soul out of sight and try desperately to ignore that something is missing they can't supply."[23] Why is it so hard to be vulnerable with others?

6. The way Francis viewed people in need changed. He began to see people with compassion rather than prejudice. How do we set aside our judgments of others?

7. Give an example of how knowing someone's story changed the way you viewed him or her.

8. Why is it so important to God for us to serve the disabled and under-resourced?

NOTES

NOTES

ENDNOTES

1. William Cowper, quoted in Alexander Campbell, *The Millennial Harbinger* (Bethany, VA: A. Campbell, 1852), 2:228.

2. C. S. Lewis, *Surprised by Joy: The Shape of My Early Life* (New York: Harcourt Brace, 1955), 221.

3. C. S. Lewis, *A Grief Observed* (New York: HarperCollins, 1961), 52.

4. C. S. Lewis, *George MacDonald: An Anthology; 365 Readings* (New York: Harper Collins, 2015), xxiii.

5. Lewis, *Surprised by Joy*, 179–80.

6. Ecclesiastes 1:9.

7. Dallas Willard, *The Divine Conspiracy: Rediscovering Our Hidden Life in God* (New York: HarperSanFrancisco, 1998), 15.

8. "Her Life at Lisieux Carmel," Society of the Little Flower, www.littleflower.org /therese/life-story/her-life-at-lisieux-carmel/.

9. "Her Life at Lisieux Carmel."

10. Saint Thérèse of Lisieux, quoted in Glenn F. Chesnut, *God and Spirituality: Philosophical Essays* (Bloomington, IN: iUniverse, 2010), 317.

11. Chesnut, *God and Spirituality*.

12. Alain de Botton, *The Architecture of Happiness* (New York: Vintage, 2008), 112.

13. Botton, *Architecture of Happiness*, 147.

14. Mark DeVries and Kirk Freeman, eds., *Augustine's Confessions* (Nashville: B&H Publishing Group, 1998), 15.

15. Augustine, *Confessions*, trans. F. J. Sheed, 2nd ed. (Indianapolis: Hackett, 2006), 37.

16. Augustine, quoted in Robin Lane Fox, *Augustine: Conversions to Confessions* (New York: Basic Books, 2015), 85.

17. Peter Brown, *Augustine of Hippo: A Biography* (Berkeley, CA: University of California Press, 2000), 101.

18. Paul R. Spickard and Kevin M. Cragg, *A Global History of Christians: How Everyday Believers Experienced Their World* (Grand Rapids: Baker Academic, 1994), 62.

19. Justo L. Gonzalez, *The Story of Christianity,* vol. 1, *The Early Church to the Dawn of the Reformation*, rev. ed. (New York: HarperOne, 2010), 247.

20. Augustine, *Saint Augustine's Confessions* (Lafayette, IN: Sovereign Grace Publishers, 2001), 1.

21. Robert West, *Saint Francis* (Nashville: Thomas Nelson, 2010), 51.

22. West, *Saint Francis*, 76.

23. Larry Crabb, *Soul Talk: The Language God Longs for Us to Speak* (Nashville, Thomas Nelson, 2003), 17.

RECOMMENDED READING

Augustine. *Confessions*. Translated by Henry Chadwick. Oxford, UK: Oxford University Press, 2008.

Botton, Alain. *The Architecture of Happiness*. New York: Vintage, 2008.

Chesterton, G. K. *Saint Francis of Assisi*. Peabody, MA: Hendrickson, 2008.

Cowper, William, and John Newton. *The Olney Hymns*. Charleston, SC: Nabu Press, 2010.

Fox, Robin Lane. *Augustine: Conversions to Confessions*. New York: Basic Books, 2015.

Gonzalez, Justo L. *Christianity*. Vol. 1, *The Early Church to the Dawn of the Reformation*. Rev. ed. New York: HarperOne, 2010.

L'Engle, Madeleine. *Walking on Water: Reflections on Faith and Art*. Colorado Springs: WaterBrook Press, 2001.

Lewis, C. S. *George MacDonald: An Anthology; 365 Readings*. New York: HarperCollins, 2015.

Lewis, C. S. *The Magician's Nephew*. New York: HarperCollins, 2009.

Lewis, C. S. *Surprised by Joy: The Shape of My Early Life*. New York: Harcourt Brace, 1955.